GREEN GRASS and WHITE MILK

From the green grass in a mountain meadow to the white milk in your cup—author-illustrator Aliki takes the young reader on a fascinating guided tour of barn and dairy. She tells how the farmer cares for his cows and what happens to the milk before it is ready to be made into cheese or ice cream.

Best of all, she gives simple step-by-step instructions for making butter and yogurt in your own kitchen. Aliki's delicious pictures are a perfect complement to this easy-to-read book about a favorite food.

For
Bruno and Camilo,
who love milk,
and
Alessandra,
who prefers buttermilk

This Is a Let's-Read-and-Find-Out Science Book

GREEN GRASS and WHITE MILK

written and illustrated by ALIKI

THOMAS Y. CROWELL COMPANY
New York

LET'S-READ-AND-FIND-OUT SCIENCE BOOKS

Editors: DR. ROMA GANS, Professor Emeritus of Childhood Education, Teachers College, Columbia University
DR. FRANKLYN M. BRANLEY, Astronomer Emeritus and former Chairman of The American Museum–Hayden Planetarium

LIVING THINGS: PLANTS

Corn Is Maize: The Gift of the Indians
Down Come the Leaves
How a Seed Grows
Mushrooms and Molds
Plants in Winter
Redwoods Are the Tallest Trees in the World
Roots Are Food Finders
Seeds by Wind and Water
The Sunlit Sea
A Tree Is a Plant
Water Plants
Where Does Your Garden Grow?

LIVING THINGS: ANIMALS, BIRDS, FISH, INSECTS, ETC.

Animals in Winter
Bats in the Dark
Bees and Beelines
Big Tracks, Little Tracks
Birds at Night
Birds Eat and Eat and Eat
Bird Talk
The Blue Whale
Camels: Ships of the Desert
Cockroaches: Here, There, and Everywhere

Corals
Ducks Don't Get Wet
The Eels' Strange Journey
The Emperor Penguins
Fireflies in the Night
Giraffes at Home
Green Grass and White Milk
Green Turtle Mysteries
Hummingbirds in the Garden
Hungry Sharks
It's Nesting Time
Ladybug, Ladybug, Fly Away Home
Little Dinosaurs and Early Birds
The Long-Lost Coelacanth and Other Living Fossils
The March of the Lemmings
My Daddy Longlegs
My Visit to the Dinosaurs
Opossum
Sandpipers
Shells Are Skeletons
Shrimps
Spider Silk
Spring Peepers
Starfish
Twist, Wiggle, and Squirm: A Book About Earthworms
Watch Honeybees with Me
What I Like About Toads
Why Frogs Are Wet

Wild and Woolly Mammoths

THE HUMAN BODY

A Baby Starts to Grow
Before You Were a Baby
A Drop of Blood
Fat and Skinny
Find Out by Touching
Follow Your Nose
Hear Your Heart
How Many Teeth?
How You Talk
In the Night
Look at Your Eyes*
My Five Senses
My Hands
The Skeleton Inside You
Sleep Is for Everyone
Straight Hair, Curly Hair*
Use Your Brain
What Happens to a Hamburger
Your Skin and Mine*

And other books on AIR, WATER, AND WEATHER; THE EARTH AND ITS COMPOSITION; ASTRONOMY AND SPACE; and MATTER AND ENERGY

*Available in Spanish

The author wishes to thank Joanna Uhry and Elmo O'Reilly for their kind help with this book.

Library of Congress Cataloging in Publication Data Aliki. Green grass and white milk. (Let's-read-and-find-out science book) SUMMARY: Briefly describes how a cow produces milk, how the milk is processed in a dairy, and how various other dairy products are made from milk.   1. Dairying—Juv. lit.   2. Milk—Juv. lit.   3. Cows—Juv. lit.   [1. Dairying.   2. Milk.   3. Cows]   I. Title.   SF239.A44   637   73-8527   ISBN 0-690-01119-9 (CQR)

4   5   6   7   8   9   10

GREEN GRASS and WHITE MILK

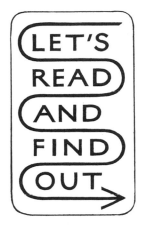

Cows graze high in the mountains
in the warm spring and summer.

They graze in valleys and in fields and meadows.
They eat and eat in good green pastures.

Nearby a farmer cuts grass.
He dries it in the sun.
He is making hay for the cold days.

In winter a cow stays in the barn, snug and warm.

She eats hay.

Good summer grass and good winter hay are healthful food for a cow.

The better a cow eats, the better milk she will give.

When a cow eats, she swallows her food quickly.
She does not chew it well.
The food is stored in the first or second of her
four stomachs.
That's right—a cow has four stomachs.

A. Unchewed food goes into stomachs 1 and 2.
B. Unchewed food (cud) is brought back up to be chewed well.
C. Well-chewed food goes into stomachs 3 and 4.
D. Part of the food is made into milk.

Later, when a cow has finished eating,
she lies quietly and chews her food again.

A cow can bring up bits of unchewed food
from her stomach.

This is called her cud.

She brings up all the food she has eaten
a little at a time.

She chews it properly and swallows it again.

That is what a cow is doing when she
seems to be chewing gum.

She is chewing her cud.

After a cow swallows her cud, her stomachs
number three and four grind the food even better.

Then part of the food is made into milk
inside the cow.

A cow begins to give milk when she has a calf.
The milk is food for the new-born calf.

A cow has milk even when her calf no longer
needs it.

So the cow's milk becomes food for us.

A healthy cow gives as much as thirty quarts
of milk a day.

Last summer I visited a farm high up in the mountains.

I went into the warm dark barn.

It smelled of straw and cows.

It smelled so much I had to hold my nose at first.

Then I got used to the smell, and I liked it.

A cow is milked twice a day.
Once in the early morning.
Once in the late afternoon.
It was the afternoon milking time.
I watched.

The cow's udder is the part
of the cow where the milk is stored.
It is a bag with four teats.
The milk comes out of them
when they are squeezed.

The cow's udder was full.

The farmer washed the cow's four teats.
Then he squeezed the teats.
He squirted some milk into a cup.
I tasted it. It was warm and good.
Then the farmer went on milking.
This milk that comes straight from the cow is called raw milk.

If a farmer has many cows, he uses a
milking machine to do the job faster.

The machine has four tubes that fit onto
the cow's teats.

The milk is pumped into a pail with a lid.

Milking by hand or by machine never hurts
the cow.

A cow feels good after she has been milked.

The farmer keeps a record of how much
each cow gives at each milking.

Then the milk is stored in a big refrigerated tank.
The tank holds milk from many cows.

Every day the milk in the farmer's tank is piped
into a tank truck and taken to a dairy.

DAIRY GARAGE

THIS WAY
TO DAIRY

MILK

RAW MILK
STORAGE
TANK

OUTSIDE

A dairy is a very clean place.
The floors and walls are spotless.
You never have to hold your nose in a dairy.

In a dairy there are pipes for the milk to
run through.
There are machines to heat and cool the milk,
and to put it into bottles or cartons.
The tanks and pipes are washed inside and
outside every night.

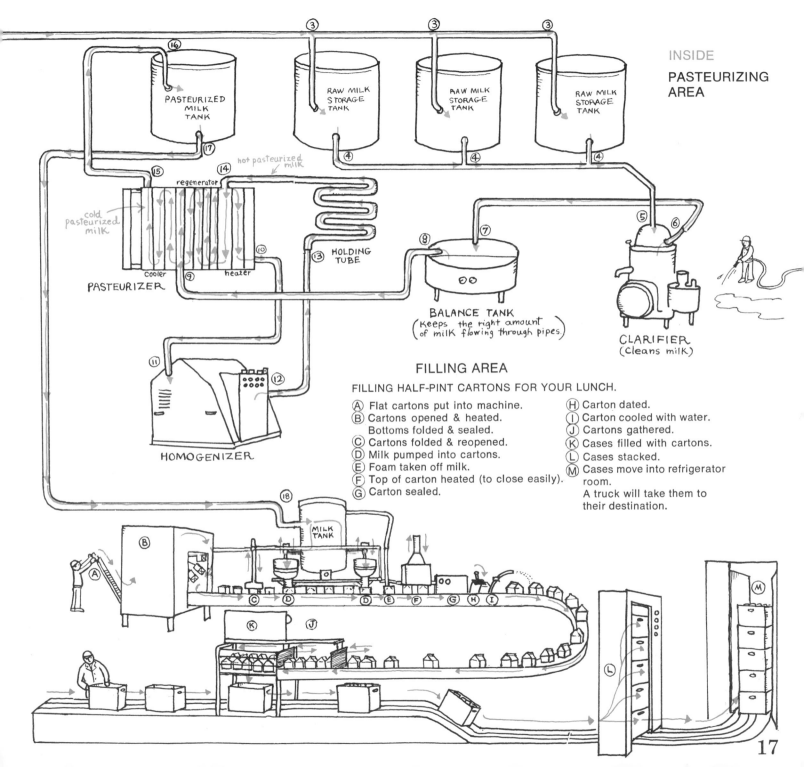

PASTEURIZED MILK TANK

RAW MILK STORAGE TANK

RAW MILK STORAGE TANK

RAW MILK STORAGE TANK

hot pasteurized milk

regenerator

cold pasteurized milk

cooler   heater

PASTEURIZER

HOLDING TUBE

BALANCE TANK
(Keeps the right amount of milk flowing through pipes.)

CLARIFIER
(Cleans milk)

HOMOGENIZER

MILK TANK

FILLING AREA

FILLING HALF-PINT CARTONS FOR YOUR LUNCH.

(A) Flat cartons put into machine.
(B) Cartons opened & heated.
  Bottoms folded & sealed.
(C) Cartons folded & reopened.
(D) Milk pumped into cartons.
(E) Foam taken off milk.
(F) Top of carton heated (to close easily).
(G) Carton sealed.
(H) Carton dated.
(I) Carton cooled with water.
(J) Cartons gathered.
(K) Cases filled with cartons.
(L) Cases stacked.
(M) Cases move into refrigerator room.
  A truck will take them to their destination.

17

When the farmer brings milk to the dairy,
it is weighed.

It is checked for freshness.

It is checked for butterfat.

Butterfat is the cream which rises to the top
of the milk if it is left to stand.

The more butterfat milk has, the more a farmer
is paid for it.

Other things happen to milk at the dairy.

After it is checked for freshness and butterfat, the milk is pasteurized to kill any bad germs.

It is quickly heated to a temperature of 161 degrees for 15 seconds.

That is not boiling.

Then the milk is quickly cooled.

Pasteurization was discovered by Louis Pasteur (1822-1895), a famous French scientist.

Homogenizer

Much of the milk we drink today is also homogenized.
Homogenized means "The same all the way through."
The milk is put into a machine called a homogenizer
where the butterfat is broken up into tiny bits.
It is mixed into the milk.
It makes all the milk rich and creamy.
The butterfat no longer rises to the top
of the milk as cream.
The milk is homogenized.

Whole milk, with butterfat in it, is too creamy for some people.

They drink skimmed milk.

Skimmed milk has all the cream taken out.

You can also buy cream, which is the butterfat of the milk.

Skimmed milk keeps me skim. I mean slim.

Cream will make me butter-fat. I mean plump.

In a dairy, milk is put into bottles or cartons.
Printed on each is the kind of milk inside.
What kind do you have at home?

"Vitamin D homogenized-pasteurized milk.
400 U.S.P. units vitamin D added per quart."

"Pasteurized skimmed milk"

"Pasteurized - Homogenized fortified lowfat milk.
2% butterfat nonfat milk solids added."

MILK

Other products are made from milk in a dairy.

Milk has proteins, vitamins, and minerals that give you energy and make you strong.

Most of the milk we drink comes from cows.
But goats, sheep, and other mammals also give milk.
In some countries where there aren't many cows,
children drink the milk of goats and sheep.

Farmers make cheese out of milk from goats and sheep.
It is very good.

Long ago people made butter
in a butter churn.

You can make butter yourself **from** cream.
Pour about half a pint of heavy cream into a big bowl.
Beat it.

First it will turn into whipped cream.
Keep on beating.
It will change.
Part of it will become watery,
and part will be little pale yellow lumps.
Pour out the water.
Spread the rest on bread.

You can make your own yogurt.
You will need:

One quart of milk

One whisk or beater

One half pint store-bought plain yogurt

One tablespoon

Two bowls

Six small jars

One strainer

1) In a large saucepan, bring the milk to a boil.
Turn off the heat. Let the milk stand for about twenty minutes.

2) When the milk is just lukewarm—
not hot and not cool—

3) . . . Strain half of it into the large bowl.
Strain the other half into the smaller bowl.

We have to work fast or the milk will get too cool!

4) Put three tablespoons of yogurt into the small bowl.
Beat it well until the yogurt is mixed with the milk.

5) Pour that bowlful into the large bowl of milk.
Mix them together well.

mixing is important!

My hand is getting stiff.

29

6) Fill each jar.

7) Put the jars in a warm place where they won't get chilled.

8) Cover the jars with wax paper and then put a small, warm blanket or bath towel over them.

9) DO NOT TOUCH or peek at the jars for at least six hours. Overnight would be better.

10) When you uncover the yogurt, it should be thick enough to eat with a spoon.

You can eat it plain, or with sugar or honey mixed in it.
Or you can put it on fresh fruit.

It's funny.
I know milk comes from cows, sheep,
and goats that eat grass.

But grass is green and milk is white.
I wonder how that happens, don't you?

ABOUT THE AUTHOR-ILLUSTRATOR

Aliki worked in many phases of the art field before she began illustrating and writing children's books. Now, when she is not too busy with books, she makes puppets and scenery for the family puppet theater, weaves baskets, and macrames.

Aliki Brandenberg grew up in Philadelphia and graduated from the Philadelphia College of Art. With her husband, Franz Brandenberg, and their children, Jason and Alexa, she now lives in New York. She and her family spend their summers among the cows in the Swiss Alps and other places.